THE YARD OUT
31-DAY DEVOTIONAL
& PRAYER JOURNAL

a Prisoners For Christ Publication

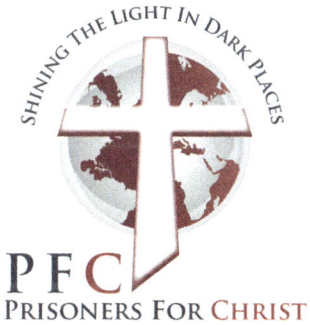

Prisoners For Christ
Outreach Ministries
P.O. BOX 1530
Woodinville, WA 98072

Cover Artwork:
"Power Of Prayer: The Lion's Den"
by Daniel in Pennsylvania

© 2023 by Prisoners For Christ Outreach Ministries, Woodinville, WA
All rights reserved.

No part of this publication may be reproduced, stored in a retrieval system, or transmitted in any way by any means — electronic, mechanical, photocopy, recording, or otherwise — without the prior permission of the copyright holder, except as provided by US copyright law. Scripture references taken from the following translations:

New American Standard Bible (NASB)
New American Standard Bible®, Copyright © 1960, 1971, 1977, 1995, 2020 by The Lockman Foundation. All rights reserved.

New International Version (NIV)
Holy Bible, New International Version®, NIV® Copyright ©1973, 1978, 1984, 2011 by Biblica, Inc.® Used by permission. All rights reserved worldwide.

New King James Version (NKJV)
Scripture taken from the New King James Version®. Copyright © 1982 by Thomas Nelson.
Used by permission. All rights reserved.

Limit of Liability/disclaimer or warranty: The publisher, author, and its agents, have used their prudent and best efforts in the preparation of this literary work, white paper, or book. They make no representations or warranties with regards to the accuracy or completeness of the contents of this literary work, white paper, or book, and specifically disclaim any implied warranties for any particular purpose. No warranty may be implied, created, or extended by any such sales or marketing representations or materials created now or in the future. The advice, strategies, or counsel contained within this literary work, white paper or book may not be suitable for the reader's specific situation. The reader accepts full and total responsibility for seeking their own personal advice or counsel on any particular matter found within.

The publisher, author or their agents shall not be liable for damages arising from the use, implementation or execution of strategies, ideas or concepts found within this literary work, white paper, or book. The fact that any organization, group, or website referenced in this literary work, white paper, or book as a footnote, (citation) or source for further information or research, does not imply that the publisher, author, or their agents endorse the information or recommendations from such organization, group, or website. Further, readers should understand and be aware any internet websites listed, may have changed, edited, or eliminated their material or even disappeared from the internet from the time of this work being published or read.

Although the publisher, author or its agents have made every prudent effort to ensure the information and authenticity of the material presented and contained within this work was correct at press time, they do not assume, hereby disclaiming any liability to any party for any such loss, damage, or disruption caused by errors or omissions, whether such errors or omissions result from negligence, accident, or any other cause.

"The Yard Out 31-Day Devotional & Prayer Journal" ISBN: 9798373289580

PFC Resource Order Form

Use this form *or* write us a letter to order free Christian resources from PFC.

- ☐ Bible Study Correspondence School
- ☐ Christian Pen Pal (*non-romantic*)
- ☐ PFC Study Bible (*NKJV*)
- ☐ Yard Out Newspaper

- ☐ Discipling Brochures and/or Tracts
- ☐ Books by PFC President & Founder, Greg Von Tobel
- ☐ Christian Literature
- List topic(s) of interest: _____
  _____

About This Devotional...

The catalyst for *The Yard Out 31-Day Devotional & Prayer Journal* was the vision of one of PFC's staff members who wanted to create something special for the "Inside Church" following the release of *The Prisoners For Christ Study Bible*. The idea was to take the wealth of inmate art, testimonies, and poetry that we have on hand from the *Yard Out* newspaper and create a full-sized, in-color devotional - like a *Yard Out* coffee table book. Along with the *Yard Out* content, several of the PFC staff wrote thoughtful devotions to include with each day's entry. The PFC staff who wrote these devotions include former prisoners, recovery leaders, in-prison volunteers, and the *Yard Out* editor, Peyton Burkhart.

In this devotional, you will find 31 days of devotions, each one containing a testimony or poem from a prisoner, a relatable Bible verse, a staff devotion, and a piece of artwork from a *Yard Out* reader. We tried to utilize as many color pieces of art as possible, since they are published in black and white in the *Yard Out* newspaper. It is amazing to see the vibrant colors and rich textures in these pieces that talented prisoners made with limited resources. Perhaps you will even recognize some of the art from previous issues of *Yard Out*. After you read each day's devotion, you are invited to write down your thoughts and prayers in the journal that follows the 31 devotions.

It is our prayer that this devotional, along with **The PFC Study Bible** and other free resources we offer, will be a blessing to you, and that it will strengthen and equip you for the good work God has planned for you (Jeremiah 29:11; Philippians 1:6). This is our gift to you - our brothers and sisters of the Inside Church. God bless you, guide you, and keep you safe.

- The Prisoners For Christ Staff

"Students of the Word" by Timothy in Alabama

"Feed My Sheep" by Bruce in Delaware

Offended Head To Toe

DAY 1

"Therefore, if anyone is in Christ, the new creation has come: The old has gone, the new is here!" 2 Corinthians 5:17 NIV

Locked away and left to rot, I was the one happiness forgot. I was fresh on a 20-year sentence at a maximum-security prison, with so many reasons to give up hope. I blamed the world for the time I got. At the time, happiness was what I was missing and searching for.

But our Lord was just getting started, showing me what true happiness comes with salvation. I didn't know it then, but my life as a child of darkness was about over and my new birth was at hand.

I have this dear friend named Kenny who is strong in faith and a servant of the Lord. He had been after me for some time to join him at church services.

Then the Lord put it (on my heart) to attend the service. I went to that chapel full of unhappiness and pity for myself. Lucky for me, that chapel only had room for love and peace that can come with faith in Jesus. I would come to learn that through my friend Kenny.

He was a peer worship leader and would co-lead with the pastor with both a message and in song. He stood at the pulpit full of love and joy and anyone could see it flowed out of him freely.

Boy, I was not happy about that at all. I was offended from head to toe and could not focus on a word said that whole service. I was dumbfounded by someone being so happy who was serving a life sentence and was locked in the same cage I was (locked in) but for longer.

The end of the service was near, and the pastor gave an altar call. It was the one piece of the service I can recall. I thought to myself, "I would take Jesus if I could be as happy as Kenny."

But I didn't say a word, nor did I have to, because the Lord knew my heart was ready. Kenny came over at the end of the service. He knew just what to say. He asked if I wanted to take Jesus as my Lord and Savior. I paused, and he asked, "Don't you want to be happy?" I did, and I took Jesus as my Lord.

Since that day, the Lord went right to work on me. He helped me lose 140 pounds. He took me from being illiterate—not even knowing the alphabet—up to the level where I could write this testimony without help. I learned to read and write by God guiding me to take 40 Bible study courses by correspondence. Amen, all glory to God.

By Bruce in Rhode Island

Transformation of the human heart is a specialty of Jesus. The Apostle Paul writes in 2 Corinthians 5:17 "Therefore, if anyone is in Christ, the new creation has come: The old has gone, the new is here!" An unhappy inmate in a maximum security prison, was ready to give up hope. He blamed the world for his circumstance. A friend reached out to share Jesus. He became a new person, educated, happy and physically fit. Positive changes always happen when people take "Jesus as Lord."

What changes do you see in your life as a result of following Jesus?

"Country Church" by Curtis in Texas (made with ink; water colors for stained glass)

No Sweeter Life

"Now that you have been set free from sin... the benefit you reap leads to holiness and the result is eternal life." Romans 6:22 NIV

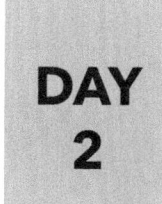

DAY 2

I was twenty-one when I caught a ten-year prison sentence. After I received my time, I recall looking around the courtroom and seeing no one there that would support me.

It's a feeling of utter hopelessness and abandonment when your mother and your pregnant girlfriend won't stand by you through the worst.

The years that followed would prove the devil had a hold on me. I was mixed up in gangs at a young age and my lack of wisdom and experience in how prison politics function would land me back in court facing distribution charges.

I was sentenced to two more years. With only the devil to guide me, it made me coldhearted. I hated the world. After nine months of being incarcerated I found out that the baby my girlfriend had promised was mine wasn't mine after all.

When you are locked in an eight by ten-foot cage, pain is hard to escape. It's hard to face yourself as a human being, and harder yet to accept it. I didn't understand until later in life that pain and anger kept me from God's sheltering hands.

Before I had tried several times to get right with the Lord. The Word says, "God is love." Whoever does not know love does not know God. But God had plans for me yet.

He sent an angel in the form of an older woman who took me in as her son and preached to me about how God granted me peace and fulfillment.

I forgave those in my life whom I felt wronged me. Her acts showed me there is still love and kindness left in the world. I let down walls built to protect myself, walls I hid my emotions behind.

This led to my newly found relationship with God through my Savior Jesus Christ. I testify to you, as a man who has been through the wringer, there is no life sweeter than a Christian Life.

By Joshua in Virginia

Loneliness isolates people from help needed to overcome hopelessness and despair. A Satanic inspired hatred trapped an inmate in pain he couldn't escape; until a Christian preached to him about God's peace and forgiveness. In the book of Romans 6:22, Paul writes, "Now that you have been set free from sin... the benefit you reap leads to holiness and the result is eternal life." Finally, he realized God's plan freed him to see love and kindness in the world.

Does being a Christian enable you to see more peace in your circumstance?

"He's Got The Whole World In His Hands" by Laurie in Missouri

Won't Trade God For Anything

DAY 3

"Draw near to God and He will draw near to you."
James 4:8 NKJV

When I was a child, I was always glad Sunday came. I loved going to church. I believed in God but never worshiped Him because I blamed God for letting my father rape me.

I moved out and got married to a man who beat me. I had two children by him. One day I fell to my knees and asked God why I let him do this to me. I heard a voice say, "That is enough," and it was because my husband got put in jail. (When he got out) I moved back; I was so in love with him, and he never hit me again. We went on with life until something tragic happened.

I lost a child, and after that, I found out I had cancer. I got so angry with the world that I started using crack cocaine. I wrote bad checks and sold drugs. I got caught and arrested. When I came to prison, I hated everyone including God.

In 2012, I was asked to go to church (to a weekend program called Kairos). I said no. The person who asked me wouldn't take no for answer. So, I went. When I walked in this room, the Holy Spirit came right into my heart. I have never felt that way in my life. The women showed me how to love again, and I got saved. I now have God with me, and I would not trade Him for anything. He is back in my life. I will never turn my back on Him. He is awesome.

I'm still with my husband, and my family started church and are God's children. God is showing the way He wants me to be. Don't give up because God will show you how to live His way.

By Mellody in West Virginia

It can be hard to understand why God allows such painful things into our lives. It's tempting to blame God and run from Him. Don't give into the lies of the enemy that keep you from your Heavenly Father. When you feel most like running from Him that is the time to run to Him and hold on tightly.

Are you holding on to Him in both good times and bad?
James 4:8, "Draw near to God and He will draw near to you."

"Even In Prison Lord" by Eliezer in (state unknown)

A Priceless Gift

"Trust in the LORD with all your heart, And lean not on your own understanding; In all your ways acknowledge Him, And He shall direct your paths." Proverbs 3:5-6 NKJV

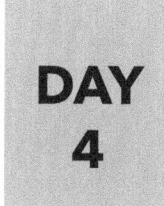

DAY 4

I was always curious about God. Like many people, I had doubts about an almighty God. But I was young and had nobody to lead me towards Him. No one in my family is religious. I had to find God on my own. In the end, it was not me that found Him. He found me.

When I was 15, I started using drugs. By the time I turned 16, I was using hard drugs with my brothers, my sisters, and even my own mother. To support my drug habit, at the age of 20, I committed an armed robbery. I robbed a 75-year-old man for his prescription medication. That crime landed me in prison for ten years.

It may sound crazy but I'm happy I was convicted and sent to prison. If I hadn't been locked up, I believe I would have died on the streets. If I hadn't been arrested, I wouldn't have been given this priceless gift.

Upon my arrival in the prison system, I was a violent individual. I ended up joining a gang and I ended up stabbing another inmate over a game of cards. But God works in mysterious ways. It's a miracle He even found His way into my life.

I was housed in a dormitory with 150 other inmates. The guy who slept in the bunk next to me read his Bible all day every day, and he prayed by his bunk every morning and night. One day, I don't know what came over me, I asked him about God.

He smiled and told me we are friends of God and can be (adopted) as sons of God, servants of God, ambassadors for and members of Christ's body. I felt at that moment I had to know more. I believe that is exactly when I received that priceless gift when Jesus took my heart in His hands.

My new friend suggested I sign up to attend church service, and I did just that. Before I had never been to church, or even stepped foot in a church. But when I went, I loved it. That same night, I signed up to be baptized, and I invited Jesus into my life.

It finally made me realize that my life needed a Savior. These years in prison have been the most amazing years of my life. Every time I open my Bible, I have an overwhelming sense of love and joy.

Jesus Christ found a way into my life. He turned me from the power of Satan. He opened my eyes from darkness to light, and I received forgiveness of my sins. Submitting myself to God every day, I finally have peace. I am blessed with a priceless gift.

By Cody in Maryland

"Trust in the LORD with all your heart, And lean not on your own understanding; In all your ways acknowledge Him, And He shall direct your paths." (Proverbs 3:5-6) A drug habit and armed robbery led a 20-year-old youth to prison. God found a way to use prison to bring a soul from darkness to the light. He received the Savior and the priceless gift of Eternal Life.

Do you plan your own roadmap or pray for God to lead the decisions you make?

"Come to the Cross" by James in Texas

God, Why Did This Happen?

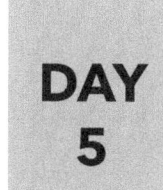

"And we know that God causes all things to work together for good to those who love God, to those who are called according to His purpose." Romans 8:28 NASB

From the day I was born, my parents dedicated me to God. As a child of God, I went in and out of jails ministering to inmates. I always wondered what it was like to be trapped in prison. Well, here I am in prison, looking out, not in.

I took a man's life out of self-defense because, being attacked, I feared for my life. I tore myself to pieces about what happened to me and what happened—that another man died. I screamed and called out to God, asking, "Why did this happen?"

Then the Holy Spirit fell upon me and (touched) the anger and rage I had for not forgiving myself. The Holy Spirit spoke to me and said, "Grab your Bible and open to Matthew 11:28." So I did and right there came my answer. It said, "For my yoke is easy and my burden is light." Right then I repented all my sins and asked God to forgive me. I needed to forgive myself for everything that happened and cast my heavy burdens and heavy yoke upon Him.

So, I gave God my all-and-all. Yes, this brought me to prison. While I'm in prison, I have peace and joy, and found my ministry where I am looking out for people who come into a mess and walk out free and clear from their sins and free from their burdens. We ought to be content and accept what is, casting our cares to God. Believing and following Him will start bigger blessings.

By Lonnie in Pennsylvania

People dedicated to God are not immune from the fallen world. Stuff happens and sometimes a law is broken, but God can redeem even the harshest circumstances. Consider this inmate who cried out to God for answers. He received an unexpected calling to minister to others caught in the same situations. Giving God his life brought peace, joy and great blessings. Paul taught the Romans in 8:28, "And we know that God causes all things to work together for good to those who love God, to those who are called according to His purpose." Many who embrace this truth have found freedom from the burden of sin as a result.

Has your attitude of surrender to God ever led you to greater blessings?

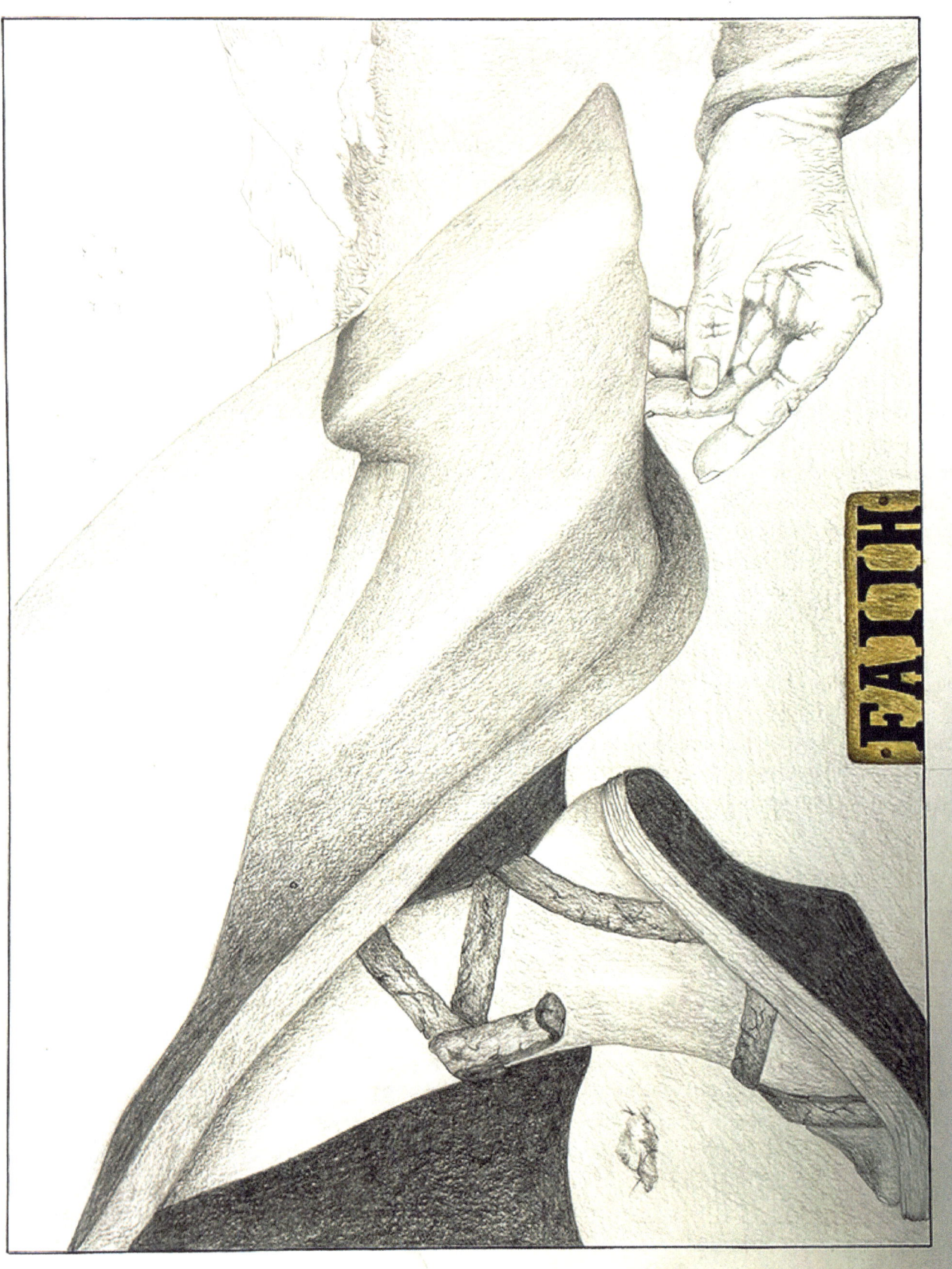

"FAITH" by Richard in New Jersey

A Heroin Addict's Recovery And Miraculous Healing

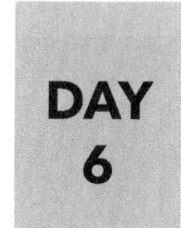

DAY 6

"He heals the brokenhearted and binds up their wounds."
Psalm 147:3 NKJV

I read Yard Out newspaper and it really touches me to know there are lots of people who have relatable stories. I came from a physically abusive family, a very bad environment. I've been in and out of jail since I was 13, and I'm 37 years old (now).

When I was 10, I would run to Sunday school and come home to the same thing—(being) left at parks from 8am to 11pm while my parents drank with their friends. At the park all day, I took care of two brothers younger than me. We were awfully hungry (and) I started shoplifting so my brothers could eat.

I got to the point where I didn't care anymore. I started using heroin at 22. I always had the Lord in my thoughts. But anger, fear, and hatred held me back from calling out to Him. But when I started using dope, I didn't want to live. I did 20 cc's of cocaine in my neck. That was my first time ever using a drug, and I didn't even smoke or drink.

My habit got to $300 a day. The last time I used drugs, I heard a voice speak to me as I loaded the rig with coke and heroin—what we called a speed ball. It was like 50 cc's. My tolerance was so high by then.

As I was going to slam, I heard someone say, "Don't do it," in a very soft voice. On my other shoulder I heard, "Yes, do it." I looked in the mirror and didn't even recognize the Lydia I was, dropping from 240 pounds to 104 pounds in six months.

I looked at the rig, and it told me again, "Don't do it." I knew in my heart it was Jesus talking to me. And I knew Satan tried to destroy me, so I broke the rig and flushed it down the toilet.

Three days later I couldn't walk at all. Kicking dope, (I was) throwing up, chills all over, like my body was begging for drugs. I was put in the hospital because I wasn't able to walk. The doctors said I could have died if I'd waited one more day. But they did say I had to get my right leg amputated because the heroin mixed with cocaine-deteriorated my hip bone. I had to sign a consent form to have my leg cut off.

But I didn't give up on the Lord, not since I was little. One night I looked up to heaven and said, "Dear Lord Jesus, I know I haven't been the person you've been trying to get a hold on, but Lord, I ask you to come into my heart. I believe your son died on the cross for me. He shed innocent blood for me. Please Lord, I repent of my sins. Please don't let them take my leg." And that very moment, I felt this peace, this comfort, as if I was crying in my mother's arms, but it was Jesus.

I got up, used both hands to throw my leg over the hospital bed, grabbed my walker and just tried and tried to walk until I started walking.

The next day my doctor came in and says, "Are you ready?" I said, "No, I'm not. The Lord has restored my leg." I got up and started walking. My doctor and the nurses stared with their mouths wide open. The Lord restored my leg, my health, and I'm walking again.

Doing time, I received this Yard Out magazine. And it really touched me. I walk with the Lord. He is so good. He is the only way. One of the poems the Lord has given me says (in part), "So let's do our time as best we can. It can't be worse 'cause with Jesus we stand."

By Lydia in Washington

This testimony shows an amazing miracle of physical healing. Praise God! More amazing still, is the miracle of a healed heart, made whole and restored. God may not always choose to heal our physical wounds but He can and will heal our spiritual sickness so we can be in a personal relationship with Him.

Have you given your soul and heart to our perfect Heavenly Father to heal?

"Never Too Late for Forgiveness" by Stephen in Pennsylvania

Chronic Relapser Breaks Addiction

DAY 7

"But as it is written: 'Eye has not seen, nor ear heard, Nor have entered into the heart of man the things which God has prepared for those who love Him.'" I Corinthians 2:9 NKJV

I was in the grip of drug addiction and on the verge of losing complete control, using and selling drugs. I had battled addiction for some 30 years, in and out of treatment centers and prison. I was once told by a counselor I was a chronic relapser and that I would never get well; and that I would likely die a lonely death in my addiction.

So, I spent the next three decades poisoning myself and every person I came in contact with. I was on bond for a dope case in one state when I was picked up for another dope case in a different state. I was miserable and looking at a possible 72 years in Nevada, and I still had the original case in Arizona. I felt my life was over and I would die in prison.

Sitting in the county jail in Vegas, I had a strong desire to read the Bible. I had cried out to God before, but who doesn't when in trouble, right? By this time, depression was starting to set in. Some weeks later, the day officer called inmates to church. Now out of 150 to 200 people, I was the only one (lining up) at the slider. I thought that was strange, but the Lord had started to work on my behalf. I thought maybe people from different parts of the jail would be there. But I was the only one. The D.O. told me to hold on, to see if the (preacher) wanted to have church since there was only one inmate.

Immediately, I thought if he is sent from God, it won't matter if there is one person or a thousand. So, this man of God invited me in the room and for the next two and a half hours we went through Scripture. I poured out my heart to him and gave my life to Jesus.

It seemed like I cried for hours in there. God heard my prayer and cry for help, and those 72 years went down to 12 years, down to 4 years. At my sentencing, the judge gave me a suspended sentence and three years' probation. Shortly after, I was extradited to Arizona where my faith was tested. I found myself in prayer about situations I usually tried to fix myself.

I beat the initial charge and was found guilty of a lesser charge. I was able to see God's mercy at every turn. God is bigger than any problem I have ever faced. What Jesus has done for me gives me a peace that surpasses anything I have ever encountered. I could go on and on about Jesus, about how He gives hope and has a plan for every life. His Word will accomplish it.

By David in Arizona

What happened to a self-professed drug addict who went to a prison chapel service where no one else showed up? He encountered Jesus in such a profound way it reversed 30 years of addiction and the onset of depression. The fact that God dramatically reduced his prison sentences was an added blessing. "'Eye has not seen, nor ear heard, Nor have entered into the heart of man the things which God has prepared for those who love Him.'" (1 Cor. 2:9) He learned no situation is bigger than God's Mercy.

In what unique ways have you experienced God's divine intervention in your life?

"In The Midst" by Ronnell in (state unknown) (made with pastels)

Loved Ones Wanted To Help

DAY 8

"The Lord himself goes before you and will be with you; he will never leave you nor forsake you. Do not be afraid; do not be discouraged." Deuteronomy 31:8 NIV

As I was growing up, the guys (and girls) I went to school with were dying off left and right. For some it was overdosing, some suicide, others from car accidents. The lucky ones ended up in jail. In high school, all my friends either drank or did drugs. I wasn't any different from anyone else. It was the cool thing to do.

Yes, there were kids getting in trouble, but not me. I was drinking, but also doing what I needed to do. I even graduated. I had and kept a job to support myself and my drinking and drug habit. Life seemed to go by really fast. I tried to start a family and spent the next eight years serving what I thought was a good cause.

In the end, it caused me more pain, and I turned to alcohol and meds to try and make it better. In reality, it only made things worse. I turned away from loved ones and friends who wanted to help. I even turned away from my Lord.

For so long, I hid behind alcohol and refused to face the demons inside. I knew what I had to do, but the devil was telling me otherwise. I couldn't let go of my past and the sins I committed. Heck, even my loved ones and my few friends forgave me. Even though the Lord did, I just couldn't forgive myself. I turned further away and drank even more.

Yet our Lord never left me. He put His shield over me and kept me alive through many things that should have killed me. Though I couldn't hear Him, He was always talking, telling me my work here wasn't done.

He told me He was going to use this, and that I am not alone. My Lord and Savior is now with me always. For the first time in 30 years, I am sober. For the first time in even longer, I am hearing Jesus.

He tells me He loves me and forgives me, and He will never stop doing either. However, He chooses to use me for the rest of my life is fine with me. How He does that will only be for the good of others.

Humans are endlessly complicated, frail, and stubborn. Not only do we bear the image of God, we also are like one another, "the good, the bad, and the ugly." It sometimes seems like we are doomed to repeat the mistakes of the past. What is true and more powerful than our never-ending opposition to the Holy Spirit is God's grace toward us.

Thank goodness that God possesses an endless supply of mercy and grace. The first step in stopping the cycle of hard-heartedness is unstopping our ears and truly opening ourselves to God's abundant love.

By Charles in West Virginia

Statistics are problematic. They don't tell the personal story behind the numbers. Overdoses, suicides and car accidents took a heavy toll on the friends and classmates of an inmate from West Virginia. His own alcohol and drug habit kept him scrambling to pay for his lifestyle. Failure and pain drove him further away from family, friends and God. But the Lord never left and even protected him from danger. Clearly, one of God's promises held true. "The Lord your God goes with you; he will never leave you or forsake you" (Deuteronomy 31:8). Through forgiveness, he discovered God's grace in a greater measure.

Are you aware God's love has never turned away from you? Think of some examples.

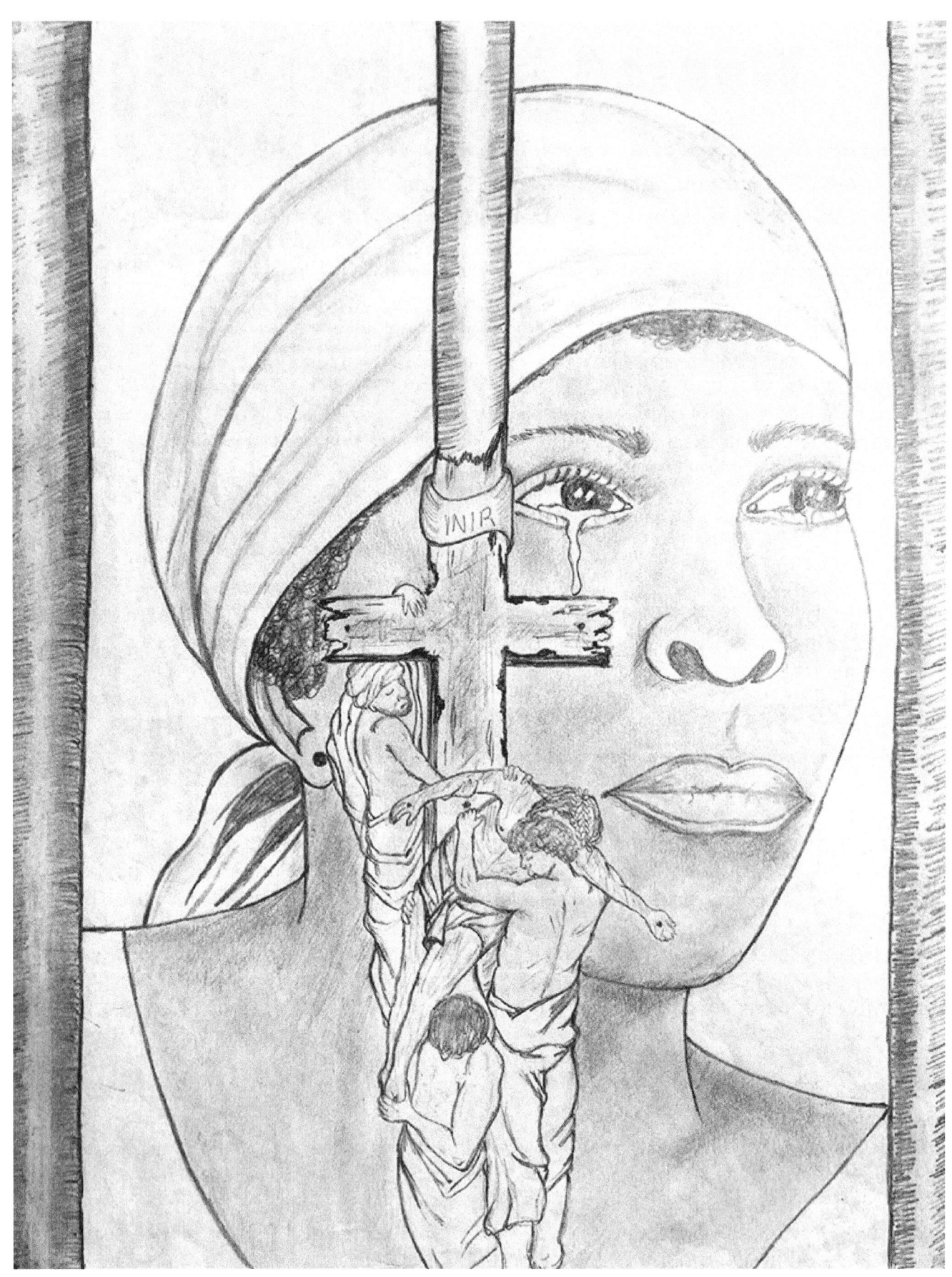

"Who Am I To Complain" by Constance in Florida

Tired And Broken Inside

"Let us therefore come boldly to the throne of grace, that we may obtain mercy and find grace to help in time of need."
Hebrews 4:16 NKJV

Before I surrendered my life to Christ, I was out running the roads, stealing and taking pills. The demon of addiction had control of my life. I knew I was going to die young if something didn't change. After hitting rock bottom and getting arrested for felony charges for the second time, I knew I had enough.

I was tired and broken inside. Jesus was the only one who could change me. Before I got arrested, I would look in the mirror and see beauty on the outside but on the inside, I felt dead and Satan was telling me my life was almost over. I might as well give up.

I was hopeless and out of control in my addiction. I was 19 years old when I felt that way. Now I am more whole than I've ever been. I am delivered from drugs. My family is being restored in my life.

I spent ten months in the county (and) constantly prayed for God to give me a clean heart. He showed me that I was bound with unforgiveness of my past. My past was keeping me entangled because I couldn't forgive myself.

I surrendered to His will and forgave myself and let go of the burdens in my heart. I felt a weight lift off of me and from that moment I began to move forward in my personal relationship with Jesus. He told me that I needed to be thankful I was in jail, because He put me here to save my life. Every day is a new day, and don't get me wrong, God never said it would be easy living for Him, but it is worth it. Jesus is definitely worth it.

Without Jesus, I would never have been given the opportunity to get my life together. My family would have had to bury me at a young age, and I would have spent eternity in hell. I know this because when I was in county, the Lord showed me a vision while I was in prayer.

I saw myself in the front of my dad's church, in a casket with my family members standing around me. I said, "God, why are you showing me this?" He said, "If you would not have turned to me, this would have been you." Jesus has changed my life forever. All things have become new. When you go through trials, listen to the Lord. Obey God and leave the consequences to Him. He is the only one who can transform us from the inside out. Even when you don't feel like your purpose is being fulfilled, stand on the promises of God. Even on our worst days, He loves us and will never give up on us.

By Taylor in Florida

We often try many useless things to "fix" ourselves, to fill our empty hearts. It is only when we realize that Jesus, and Jesus alone, is the only One who can complete us and make us whole that we will truly be alive, not just existing but alive! Jesus understands our frailties and stands ready to forgive and restore us when we fall.

Have you filled your empty heart with the love of Jesus and accepted His gift of grace and forgiveness so you can come alive in Him?

"Coming To Truth" by Charles in Michigan

How Much More Can I Handle?

"...Do not fear, for I have redeemed you; I have called you by name; you are Mine!" Isaiah 43:1 NASB

My name is a number. I reside at a state prison. However, I am freer in my life today than I have ever been. I know you're thinking I'm crazy. How can someone be free in prison? If you take a moment to listen to my testimony, I'll tell you.

In March of 2014, I was sitting outside a motel bar in the parking lot. I had just done enough alcohol and drugs to kill a horse or two, just to feel what I thought was normal. My thinking was so disturbed. I was a shell of a man with a heart of stone, ready for action as always.

Instead of saying my normal prayer like, "Lord don't let me be caught tonight," or whatever disturbed thought I had—I simply looked at the sky and said, "I don't know how much more I can handle, Lord. I'm lost. Please let Your will be done through me."

Within twenty minutes, I was rescued, not arrested. I know today that humble simple prayer saved my life and soul. I could tell you all the war stories that got me here.

But there is no need. To move on, we must let go of the past. If not, we will remain in the same old story over and over, as I have all through life. Being in prison today took a lot of time and effort. I have been on both sides of the smoking gun many times.

But look around, look at where you are. It's not the end of the world.

Be still, listen before it's too late, and you will hear. It will take time and effort. But the reward is a serenity that can't be bought. I walk around this prison waiting to be extradited to another state to do more time there.

To take advantage of this gift freely given to you, humble yourself today. There's a new future for us all. Will you find it or go against the grain? Please make the right choice. I know you can. Surrender is the key to independence.

By Joseph in Pennsylvania

Social complexity and government oversight often reduces individual life to a number. This is even more true for prisoners, whose identities orbit around an ID number. This inmate escaped the cycle to experience personal freedom. Isaiah 43:1 reinforces this belief. "...Do not fear, for I have redeemed you; I have called you by name; you are Mine!" His rescue was an arrest. The same old story got a new ending.

Has God redirected your life in a miraculous way?

"The Four Gospels" by Scott in California (made with water colors)

My Daughter's Short Life Saved Others

DAY 11

"Put on the full armor of God." Ephesians 6:11 NIV

When I was a young kid, I didn't know God. But as I was walking one night after sneaking out, I got scared of a tree shadow. I remember looking up and praying, "Lord, I want to be your soldier. I want to fight Satan." I often think about that prayer. I knew nothing of either God or Satan, but I felt safe.

By the time I was 18, I had gotten into trouble, gone to prison, and became a gangster. For thirteen years I was in and out of prison doing things that were wrong. Once I beat down a child molester really bad.

Later when I was released and moved to Arizona, I met Angela, the love of my life. She touched my heart. But by the end of that year, I was on my way back to the Department of Corrections. Angela begged me to change my life. So, I picked up a Bible—which wasn't the first time—but there was something different about it this time. It was alive.

One night in county jail, I was in a prayer circle talking about child molesters and praying for them. Then the hand of God pulled me to my knees, and I repented for the beat down, and I got saved.

I ended up back with Angela and she and I had two baby girls. Well, I got arrested and locked up again, when my youngest was only 24 days old. About three months later, my daughter died from drowning. My wife left the bathroom for just a minute, and she died. Then a true test of my faith was in front of me. While I was on the phone with my wife, I had to pull the plug on my daughter in the hospital. I prayed for strength, and I got it. I felt God's arms around me. The Lord was hugging me, and I was okay.

Filled with the Holy Spirit, I told Angela, "Baby, I love you deeply and I forgive you." We donated our baby's body parts. In our daughter's short life, she saved others. Two little kids got to live on. My wife learned about love and forgiveness, and my faith grew so much stronger.

After her death, I have been able to help many other inmates learn love and forgiveness of our Lord. I'm in Bible studies daily and every time I tell this story I see a seed being planted. I have become a light in the darkness of prison, a living testimony.

God's plan for me here is to save others, in a place where many won't go to help. I have five years to help as many as I can before my release. I went from being a gangster to knowing God, and my childhood prayer was finally answered. I'm a Soldier of God.

By Jesse in Arizona

Childhood memories often bring reflections when adults consider how the years bring a dream to reality. A kid, scared of a shadow, once prayed to be a soldier of the Lord. Then at 18, just the opposite happened. He was a prison yard gangster, in Satan's army. A phone call from his wife brought a 180 degree turn around. Learning his infant daughter drowned in the bathtub, he felt an embrace of God's arms and his faith grew stronger. He shares with others the Lord's love and forgiveness as he helps God save others. Ephesians 6:11 reminds us to, "Put on the full armor of God." In obedience, his childhood prayer was answered. "I am a Soldier of God."

How does the armor of God equip you to defeat Satan's attacks?

"Looking in the Eyes of Jesus" by Renee in Texas

God Helps

"Fear not, for I am with you; Be not dismayed, for I am your God. I will strengthen you, Yes, I will help you, I will uphold you with My righteous right hand." Isaiah 41:10 NKJV

DAY 12

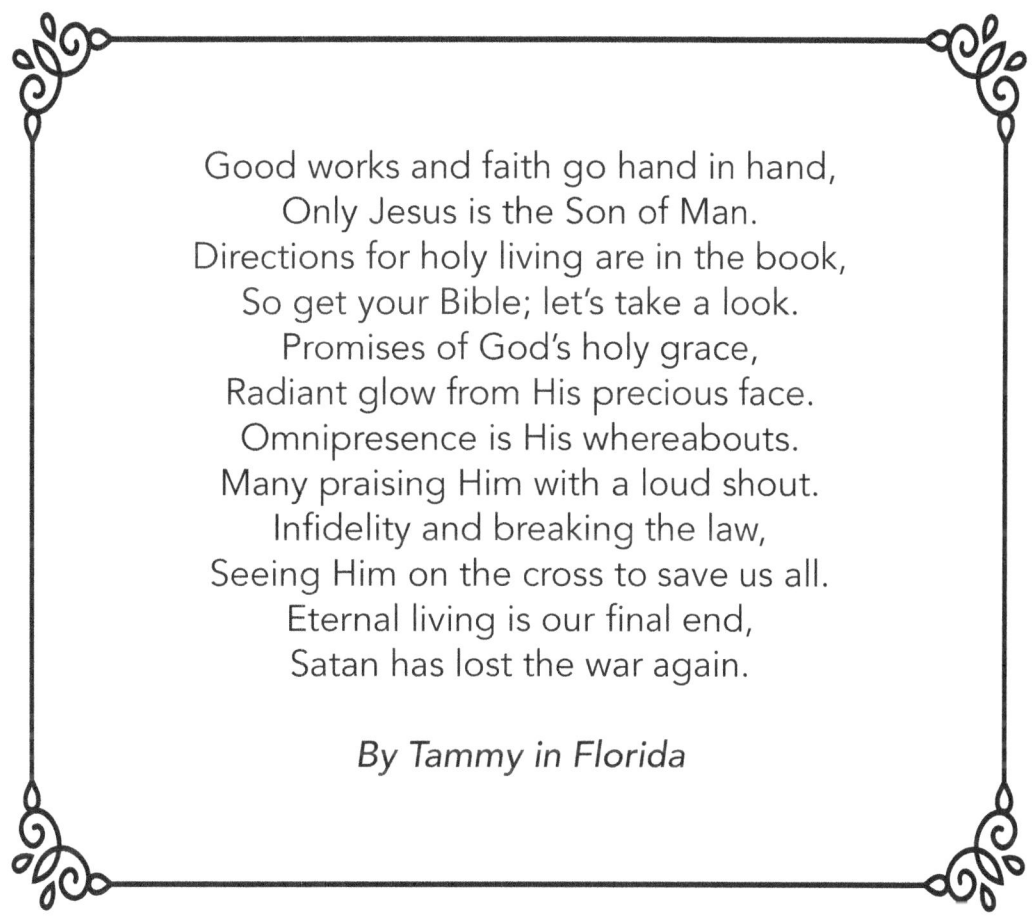

Good works and faith go hand in hand,
Only Jesus is the Son of Man.
Directions for holy living are in the book,
So get your Bible; let's take a look.
Promises of God's holy grace,
Radiant glow from His precious face.
Omnipresence is His whereabouts.
Many praising Him with a loud shout.
Infidelity and breaking the law,
Seeing Him on the cross to save us all.
Eternal living is our final end,
Satan has lost the war again.

By Tammy in Florida

What a blessing to have a Father who will always keep His promises to His Children. He promised to never leave our side. He promised to listen whenever we cry out to Him. He promised to give us His peace no matter our circumstances. He promised we can be with Him for all eternity!

People will break promises to us. We will even break promises to ourselves. God's promises to us are unbreakable!

Are you resting in the unbreakable promises of your Heavenly Father?

"Love Never Fails" by Gregory in Missouri

Nothing To Live For

DAY 13

"Truly I say to you, whoever does not receive the kingdom of God like a child will not enter it at all." Mark 10:15 NASB

When I was 18 months old, my mom left me on the front porch at my aunt and uncle's house in the middle of December. They took me under their wings and raised me.

I would sit at the front door when I was five and cry for my mom. But she never came back. I didn't understand why she did what she did. Maybe it was me. I thought I did something wrong, and that she hated me. When I turned 12, my mom would come every year to take my brother (who lived with us) out for his birthday, while she never looked at me or talked to me. She never gave me anything for my birthday or took me anywhere.

I was so hurt I wanted to take my life. I tried hanging myself, but my brother walked in and stopped me. He told my aunt. Sunday morning, my aunt asked me to go with her to church. It was Easter Sunday and I went. They were talking about how Jesus died on the cross for my sins and how He rose three days later.

When we went home my aunt told me Jesus loves me and He is always there to listen to me and help me through my struggles. That night I prayed and asked God to forgive me of my sins. I asked Him to help me have a closer relationship with my mom.

Then it hit me. I do have something to live for. Jesus put me on this earth for a reason, and I need to live for that purpose.

To this day God has worked in amazing ways. I have a close relationship with my mom, and I am sharing the amazing way God works. I thank the Lord every night for saving me and never turning His back on me and always having faith in me.

By Stephen in Pennsylvania

Painful experiences often start early in life. A young boy abandoned by his mom learned that the hard way. Neglected from an early age, grief pushed him to the brink of suicide. A supportive aunt helped him realize a relationship with Jesus. Mark 10:15 reminds us that the kingdom of God is accessible to children. He discovered new meaning and purpose in life. God even helped him grow close to his mom.

Do you have a healthy relationship with your family?
What would improve the relationship?

"Prayer, Innocence, and Temptation" by Troy in North Carolina (made with pastels on canvas)

Machines Keeping Me Alive

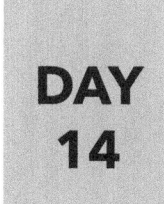

DAY 14

"And without faith it is impossible to please God, because anyone who comes to him must believe that he exists and that he rewards those who earnestly seek him." Hebrews 11:6 NIV

A lot has happened in my life from which I can definitely assure you that God does exist. Not only has He been watching and providing for me, but He has given me another chance in life.

In 2015, I was really doing much hurt to myself and died of an overdose. It was one night when I was out drinking at a bar that I decided to take something. I didn't know what it was, but I took it anyway and passed out.

While in the hospital, doctors were doing everything they could to keep me alive, but they couldn't do much.

My family members are Christians and firm believers in Christ. They began to pray for me. Doctors told them the machines were the only thing keeping me alive. I had only a 10% chance of survival.

My family was devastated and couldn't believe what they were hearing. To top it off, doctors told them they wanted to pull the plug.

My mother immediately said no. She believed God was going to save me. Being the believer she is, my mother found the hospital chapel and pleaded with God.

Whatever she said to God worked because I am alive to tell you all this testimony.

I don't know what God has planned for me, but it must be huge because He gave me another chance in life. God can do anything, especially the impossible.

So those who believe in Him, keep believing, and those who don't, I encourage you to please do so because God does exist.

By Eliezer in Rhode Island

Was it a miracle or an improbable medical healing? A praying mom knows the answer to that question. When he was on life support machines with a 10% chance to live, doctors told her they wanted to pull the plug on her son. She immediately said no. Her pleading prayers brought healing to her son and a renewed purpose with an assurance that God is real. Hebrews 11:6 reinforces that belief. "God … exists and He rewards those who earnestly seek Him."

Has anyone ever had your back in prayer?
Can you testify to a miracle answer?

"Help In The Storm" by Leartis in Georgia

Prayer Circle Support

DAY 15

"For I know the plans that I have for you, declares the Lord, plans for prosperity and not for disaster, to give you a future and a hope. Then you will call upon Me and come and pray to Me, and I will listen to you." Jeremiah 29:11-12 NASB

I heard it coming from behind me. "I didn't come at ya cuz you're in the prayer circle. Normally I woulda come at ya," said a belligerent basketball player new to the prayer circle. Well, that got my attention. She and another member were posed for a confrontation, but what came out of her mouth was nothing short of a miracle. "I didn't come at ya."

Never in my wildest dreams did I think I'd hear that conversation in the yard right after a prayer circle. Since we started the circle, we've seen lots of change in our daily lives. Many of us have known Jesus for a time. A few were just getting to know Him. And all of our lives were changing.

It began simply enough. I was in the bakery and an inmate heard me talking about prayer. She had just come to Christ, so she asked me how to pray. I told her it's a conversation with God, just talking to Him like you would a good friend. She and another friend were going to meet, so I suggested we pray together. And we decided to invite the whole unit to the yard for prayer.

It was a sunny Saturday, and 22 women gathered and formed a prayer circle in the yard. I started with a short, "Dear Lord, we come before you, standing in this circle. We ask a hedge of protection around us. We make our requests by prayer with thanksgiving." Then the woman on my right started, and one-by-one everyone went around saying what they wanted to pray.

We prayed for families, friends, situations, and circumstances. I closed with, "And for all petitions we hold in our hearts in Jesus' name we pray." As a result, we experienced a number of miracles. Family relations healed, our health improved, we gained better ability to resist the evil one, reduced sentences, charges being dropped, and a noticeable change in the power, love and self-control within us all.

At the first group, we got off to a rocky start. An inmate very loudly tried to break us up. She walked around the outside of the circle screaming, and making crude, nasty comments. I just put my right hand up and said, "Please stop." One of us added something and words were exchanged, but we did not stop. The next day we met, she didn't come around to try and stop us.

We who are in the circle support each other. We found it's an excellent way to spread the Word of God. New members are attracted to us when they see our joy and the results. Prayer circles are easy to start. Matthew 18:20 promises, "Where two or three are gathered in my name there am I in their midst." So, God is with us, and He can be with you in this way too.

By Mary in Washington

It is so beautiful to read this testimony of hope and restoration when the women of God stand together and choose unity over strife. It brings to mind one of God's promises found in Jeremiah 29:11-12. "For I know the plans that I have for you, declares the Lord, plans for prosperity and not for disaster, to give you a future and a hope. Then you will call upon Me and come and pray to Me, and I will listen to you."

God hears our prayers and blesses those who trust Him.

"Not By Might Nor By Power" by Steve in Texas

Why Am I Here On Earth?

DAY 16

"And so we know and rely on the love God has for us..." 1 John 4:16 NIV

Sometime last September I started down a slippery slope. I didn't care who I took with me. I was hurt, depressed, and so angry I couldn't sleep. I couldn't eat. I couldn't turn to anybody.

My bunkie, Jaysen, was really tired of me and one night we had a bad fight. It almost ended up with one of us moving. For three days neither of us spoke to the other. While everybody else was at dinner I started yelling, "Why am I here on earth? To be hurt? To be stepped on? Abused?" I started kicking the bathroom door and the lockers. I had enough and went out to the yard to try and clear my head. I couldn't, so I went to bed and really couldn't sleep.

Next morning, after being lower than rock bottom, something told me to pray. I looked around. Jaysen was asleep, and so were my dormies. "Pray," came the word again. So, I turned over and said, "Heavenly Father." Tears came, so I got on my knees and prayed like I've never prayed before. I reminded God, "Whatsoever you ask shall be done." As I was praying, Jaysen patted my shoulder and said, "This too shall pass." I asked God for forgiveness, for guidance, for Him to remove the depression, hurt, anger out of me, and to fill me with the joy, happiness, and the peaceful love that I now have.

While writing down what happened, God told me to get rid of my porn. I used to be gay, and God delivered me from that. I was so tired of living, I also had two strings torn from a sheet. No one would miss me. I handed them to Jaysen and told him I didn't need them anymore. He handed me a sheet of paper with words he wrote a few years ago that said, "Whatsoever you ask shall be done." Now, I have no doubt God is real.

By Chris in California

After an emotional outburst and conflict with a cell mate, an inmate hears God say "pray." Tears brought the most fervent prayer of his life. Freedom from hurt and anger led to joy, and peaceful love, leaving no doubt God is real. 1 John 4:16 reminds us, "And so we know and rely on the love God has for us..."

Does knowing God loves you deepen your spiritual connection to Jesus?

"Job 7:4" by Jamison in North Carolina

One Hour A Day

"Revive me, O Lord, for Your name's sake! For Your righteousness' sake bring my soul out of trouble."
Psalms 143:11 NKJV

DAY 17

In prison for a crime I didn't commit, I've been fighting the criminal justice system for 30 years. I used to hate God because why would He put me here? Just because I was hardheaded and didn't believe in Him? I was very angry when I came to prison.

In my mind nobody could help me, so I went to a jury trial and they found me guilty of murder. So I sold drugs, did drugs, and was very mean toward others. For fifteen years, I was angry until one person challenged me.

He said, "If you didn't do this crime, then do something about it. And I'll help you, but you must also help me. Give me one hour of your day and read Scripture with me." So I did. And I found out it was God who put me here because the lifestyle I was living was out of control.

Now I truly have changed and have done so much with my life. I became a Christian, learned to read and write, got my GED, and can't count the college classes I have taken. I learned to research law and have been back to court four times. In 2016, I filed my last and final motion with the court. A new judge granted a DNA test and appointed me counsel. Why? Because of prayer and faith, and the words, "What you sow, so shall you reap."

I did years of counseling on myself, drug treatment, and education classes. I asked God what He wanted from me. (I told Him) I will be your servant in prison, and do the work you want, or you may want me to go serve the world.

Then I got a sign. The courts tested the evidence, and now my lawyer tells me I'm going home. The evidence used at my trial in 1989 turned out to be lies. Sometime this year, I will get my sentence overturned and walk out of this prison a free man. (I may get money) for wrongful conviction.

I'll use it to help the world, like the poor, homeless, hungry, and whoever else needs help. I have nobody but me and God. I have no technology skills or the knowledge on how to use a smart phone. But two things I have for sure are God and my faith. With those two, I will move mountains.

By Herman in Nebraska

Transformation takes time but it starts with a single step. An inmate hated God, believing He was responsible for his wrongful conviction. Challenged to read the Bible, he slowly began to shift his point of view. He became a Christian, learned to read and write, and took college classes. A court appeal brought new evidence that proved his innocence, with a soon-coming prison release. A verse enhancing his experience is Psalm 143:11. "Revive me, O Lord, for Your name's sake! For Your righteousness' sake bring my soul out of trouble."

Patience allows believers to wait for God's divine intervention.
Is it easier to wait for answered prayers when we trust God?

"To God Be the Glory" by Christy in Illinois

Time For A New Chapter

DAY 18

"And take the helmet of salvation, and the sword of the Spirit, which is the word of God." Ephesians 6:17 NKJV

In my teen years I did dumb things to hang with the cool kids. As I got older my surroundings changed. Afraid to be different, I followed, not looking at the big picture. I became a busy, young mom, holding down a job and being a parent.

I thought I could hide my drug addiction from family, co-workers, and friends. Not seeing how bad my addiction became, I got out of hand, and was arrested for writing false prescriptions. I did the programs and kept my head straight for five years. New Year's Day came around and some friends said it wouldn't hurt to have a little fun. One day turned into weeks, then months and soon, I was back to the old me. This time I was selling drugs to pay for my habit.

It got easier as time went on, and so did the thought I wouldn't get hurt. Selling became my life until one night, doing my thing, I was punched in the face, beaten up and robbed. I lay helpless in a cold, dark alley, with my assailant telling me he was going to kill me.

I kept my eyes closed and prayed, "God, I need your help. I can't do this alone." I wondered how He could let this happen to me. Soon, a nurse found me in that alley early in the morning. She had just come home from work and was taking her trash out. She told me God had plans for me and that He was trying to tell me things I didn't want to hear.

God wants us to learn from our mistakes. (Understanding that, I made) Jesus Christ, my Lord and Savior. I was blessed when my chaplain handed me the Yard Out newspaper. I see that I'm not alone. Also, I'm not the only one who feels this way. We can all change.

By Angela in Connecticut

There is no other weapon against temptation except the "sword of the Spirit, which is the Word of God" (Ephesians 6:17). Colossians 3:2 tells us to set our minds on the things above, not on the things that are on earth. If our minds are filled with the majesty and holiness of God, the love and compassion of Christ, and the brilliance of both reflected in His perfect Word, we will find that our interest in the lusts of the world will diminish and disappear. Without the Word's influence on our minds, we are open to anything Satan wants to throw at us. Stand firm my sisters and brothers in Christ.

We CAN all change.

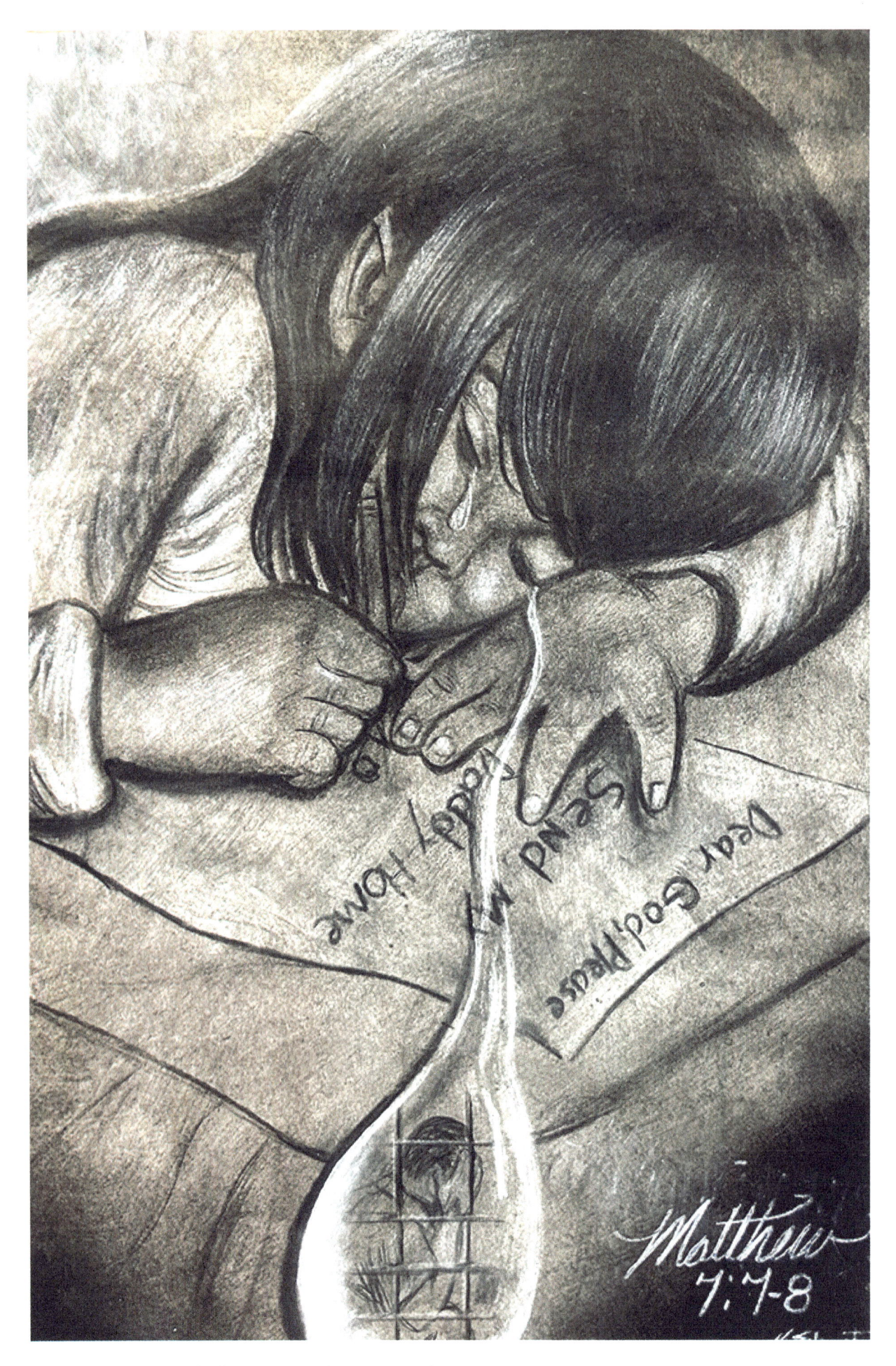

"A Letter to God" by Kennard in Pennsylvania

Life Flipped Upside Down

DAY 19

"Peace I leave with you. My peace I give to you...."
John 14:27 NKJV

I was born into a family consumed by violence and drugs. So, from the time I was a toddler until adulthood, I was surrounded by every kind of evil. Now, here I sit, nearly 40 years old and in prison for the third time. I have been in and out of facilities since the age of twelve. That sounds horrible.

As sad as that is, especially in regard to constantly leaving my children without their father, I must admit, I have peace. There are no more excuses, no more lies, no more pain, and no more substances to hide my true emotions. I am no longer selfish, but rather, selfless. I am no longer anxious but patient. I am no longer bitter or angry but gentle and kind.

No longer violent, I have become a peace maker. Prison by no means guarantees positive changes. Some may even argue it makes people worse. And as far as dealing with emotions are concerned, that was my experience every time I came home from prison.

Along with a whole lot of other factors, I became a monster. Then my life got turned upside down. What did it? I picked up my cross and followed Jesus. With all the mental trauma I suffered in life, from the murders in my family, to the verbal and physical abuse, alcohol and drug addictions, incarcerations, and the toxic relationship with the woman in my life, I was healed.

No counseling, no therapy, no medication needed. Now whether you're a believer or not, any logical person can see the fundamental teachings of Christianity are awesome—which are love, peace, joy, and servitude. In a dog-eat-dog world, Christ teaches us to put the next man first.

Like I say whether you're a believer or not, how can anyone with a clear conscience deny such a pure faith with these tangible results? No, I don't have all the answers, nor do I pretend to, but one thing I can tell you though is with dedication and obedience to the Holy Scripture and Jesus Christ, my life was transformed. And for that alone I will forever be thankful. For that alone I praise the God of the Bible.

If you are blessed to read this testimony, may His grace and peace fill your entire being. In closing, if you give true Bible teaching and Christianity a chance, your life will be transformed for the better as well. I have never felt peace and joy like this. And it is only because of Jesus. Accept Him into your life today, gain a personal relationship with Him through prayer. Read your Bible. You will not be disappointed.

By Michael in Michigan

When does an ordinary experience lead to a life changing conversion? Not that any prison fall is ordinary, but when the violence and crime keeps repeating itself, a pattern develops, and the cycle starts again. What changed for a Michigan inmate was his commitment to Jesus. His toxic behavior was healed. "No counseling, no therapy, no medication needed." His traumatic emotions were replaced by peace and joy. "Peace I leave with you. My peace I give to you...." John 14:27

Have you experienced the gift of godly peace the world cannot give?

"Shades of Grace in Graphite" by Terry in Colorado

A New Beginning

DAY 20

"He brought them out of darkness and the shadow of death, And broke their chains in pieces." Psalms 107:14 NKJV

Since I was little, I grew up in church. All my life I've heard, "God has a calling on you." But to be honest, I was never really into church. At times I would seek God because of something I was going through. But it was never really about God.

I started using pills and smoking weed when I turned 14. I was always fighting. That turned into gunfire and shoot outs. I was stealing, robbing drug dealers, selling drugs and more. If it was something negative, I was doing it.

At 16 I joined a gang. About a year later, I went to jail for robbery and was released in 30 days. In fifteen days, I was locked up for possession of a gun. I thank God I was locked up because I would have killed my dad for beating my mom. Fast forward to December 20, 2017. That day changed my life. It was the day I killed a friend for betraying me. It's the day I gave my life completely to God. I was going through so much pain from people I thought were my friends. I wanted a chance to start over.

The next day I turned myself in. I asked God to do a miracle knowing I had to stand up for what I'd done. I asked God to do a new thing in me. Immediately I began to forgive myself and forgive others. Within nine months I was sentenced to 24 years (to serve 85%). That was hard for me to hear but still after that, I remained faithful and became even closer with God.

Since being in prison, I've never felt freer. I'm at peace and I have so much hope and faith in God. No matter what they say, I know God has a purpose for me. I remain focused on God and allow Him to change me completely so I can fulfill His purpose. I am so thankful for Jesus and I'm here to tell you He loves us all.

No matter how bad it seems, never give up. Remain faithful. He's done a lot for me, and I know things are going to work out for you too.

By Shansay in New Jersey

Justice requires a balance between law and consequences. The natural order of society requires a draw down. We are not suspended in space, an entity unto ourselves. Certain lines should not be crossed without penalty. It took the worst for one inmate to realize that. He turned to God for changes and found freedom, peace and hope. Psalms 107:14 says, "He brought them out of darkness and the shadow of death, And broke their chains in pieces."

Patience allows believers to wait for God's divine intervention. Is it easier to wait for answered prayers when we trust God?

"Stairway To Heaven" by Trinity in South Carolina (made with acrylic on canvas)

The Last Time?

DAY 21

"Surely God is my help; the Lord is the one who sustains me." Psalms 54:4 NIV

As I lay down, I wonder; who else in here is awake?
Is this all an awful dream, or just a huge mistake?
No, I put myself here, I know this much is true,
for all the wrongs that I have done, and those that I still do.
Will this be my last time here, this place I've come to know?
Away from all I hold so dear, feeling sad and low.
I know I have it in me, to change my sinful deeds.
I can break this vicious cycle and see where life will lead.
I'm on a journey strange and new, but exciting just the same.
My life can be my own to live, not just a junkie's game.
And so I make this heartfelt plea, coming from my soul.
To all those who care for me, "Please help me reach this goal."
I cannot do it all alone. Regardless, I will try.
Because I know the alternative is back in jail or die.

By Kimberly in Washington

The Bible tells us that we are unable to do any good in and of ourselves (Romans 7:18-19). Therefore, we are in need of someone who is better than us who can help us be better. Of course you know that "someone" is Jesus Christ. No other name has been given to us that can save us (Acts 4:12). To the one suffering, lean on the Lord for your salvation and deliverance. To the one witnessing suffering around you, be the hands and feet of Jesus by comforting others and speaking encouragement into their situations. Although our salvation comes from above, we were not made to travel this life alone. Surround yourself with like-minded believers who will not steer you wrong. Study God's Word daily and pray for God to lead you in every aspect of your life.

"Surely God is my help; the Lord is the one who sustains me."
Psalms 54:4

"Our Father" by Jeremy in Florida *(made with coffee and tissues on paper)*

Little Crime, Big Time

DAY 22

"The sacrifices of God are a broken spirit, A broken and a contrite heart— These, O God, You will not despise."
Psalms 51:17 NKJV

Ten dollars of the devil's money took my freedom. I'm doing 8 to 13 years for being in the presence of a drug deal. Some people say, "That's not right — take it back to court," or, "That's too much time for that little crime."

But the thing was, they only knew what I told them. See, I did not tell them all the times I cursed my parents growing up. I did not tell them about the drinking and drugging. I did not tell them about the stealing of money. I only told them about me being wronged.

God has been dealing with me on the inside. I am currently locked down for various reasons, and it's here that I have peace of mind.

It's here that I am able to see my failures for what they really are. And it's here I can allow God to be God.

It's not a very good feeling being lost, because you never know what to expect, you never know what dangers await you. If we would only take time out to pray and ask for guidance.

God has allowed me to come across Yard Out, and I'm glad because I can fellowship with born-again Christians. I pray if you are reading this, know that no one said it was going to be easy.

Sometimes it gets a little tough, but that's when God gets tougher. Follow Him and He will direct your path.

by Erica in Mississippi

Erica in Mississippi has come to a realization that is so important for us as believers: We are deserving of much more punishment than we receive. Spiritually speaking, we deserve death for our sins. (Rom 6:23)

As it relates to our daily lives, how many times have we broken the law and not been caught? Some in-prison volunteers openly admit, "The only reason I'm not in prison too is because I didn't get caught." God loves this attitude from His children. We do not assume that we deserve anything good, for nothing good is in us. Therefore, all of our prideful excuses fade away to simple thankfulness that God has NOT given us what we deserve, but rather grace and mercy through His Son Jesus Christ.

Do you have any offenses that have not been accounted against you? Can you think of examples of God's grace and patience in your life while you were running from Him?

"The Prodigal Comes Home" by John in Maryland

Agree With God's View

DAY 23

"But each one is tempted when he is drawn away by his own desires and enticed. Then, when desire has conceived, it gives birth to sin; and sin, when it is full-grown, brings forth death." James 1:14-15 NKJV

For most of my adult life, I knew Jesus was my redeemer, my conqueror, and my king. However, I erroneously assumed I could call Him my Savior while remaining enslaved in the enemy's camp- held captive by sin, human philosophy, and Satan himself. I was defeated in my Christian walk. I was desperate for a victory.

So, what happened? Well, praise God, I was rescued from the enemy's clutches. "How?" you may ask. Simply put, I went to prison. Yes, prison is where I was set free. A paradox? Yes, but such is the kingdom of God.

In prison I began to hear and to listen to that "still, small voice," and I began to agree with God's view as it concerned the condition of my soul. I agreed I was poor, I was a captive, that I was blind. These were spiritual conditions from which only my rescuer could deliver me. And, hallelujah, He did.

My attitude was similar to a majority of folks. I could not see my desperate need for Jesus as my deliverer. I could not accept His assessment of me spiritually. I waited until I was physically poor, physically held captive and physically oppressed before I recognized that Jesus was not only my Savior, but equally as important, my deliverer. I was too proud and self-reliant to accept this truth.

I had come to Christ as a little seven-year-old boy. I was baptized at age thirteen. I started to fall in love with Him. But because I didn't fit the description of those whom Jesus came to set free, I was fooled into Satan's trap.

I began to be enslaved to sin. My sin was hidden from everyone. Everyone but God and me. I began to believe that my sinfulness didn't really matter since nobody knew. Then at last, Satan held me captive to do his will.

This seems to be the natural progression Satan uses to bring God's people from victory to defeat. He tempts them to sin, then gets them to believe sin is not really that bad. Finally, he has them in his clutches. That's what happened in my life.

I went from a joyous, victorious teenager who loved God with all my heart and ended up a thirty-something, devastated by the destruction sin can wreak on one who is not walking in the Spirit. I came face-to-face with the old adage: "Sin takes you further than you want to go. It keeps you longer than you want to stay, and it will cost you more than you want to pay."

Here I am, now in the thirteenth year of this sentence. As I glance back over these years, I see His hand leading and caring for me. Not only did He get my attention, He got my heart. There's nothing left for me; it's all His. I give it to Him freely, just as Christ Jesus gave His all for me.

By Mark in Missouri

Mark in Missouri confesses what James tells us in his letter, that sin carries us away and brings death (James 1:14-15). Knowing that we are sure to fail on our own, we can find hope and rest in the fact that Jesus has already secured our salvation. Even when we stray, the Great Shepherd is always near to us and will lead us back to the green grass of His protection, love, and guidance, if we will turn back to Him.

In what ways were you drawn away from God?
In what ways could you still be tempted? Be honest with yourself.

"Don't let the excitement of youth cause you to forget your creator. Honor him in your youth before you grow old and say, "Life is not pleasant anymore."

Ecclesiastes 12:1

"Youth In Praise" by Heather in Florida

My Life Was A Complete Mess

DAY 24

"Blessed are the poor in spirit, for theirs is the kingdom of heaven." Matthew 5:3 NASB

When I was about six years old, my mom and dad decided to get a divorce. It crushed me. I remember lying in bed praying to God to please bring my family back together again. Well, it never happened.

That's when I lost my faith. I started living life my way. At age 13, I robbed a record store and from there I just got worse. I started doing and selling meth and ended up in prison for three years.

When we started making meth, the cops raided my brother's house and I ended up taking the rap so that my wife, my brother, his wife, and a friend wouldn't get into trouble. I did two more years.

Then I was doing pretty good, until my mom passed away. I had about three months left on parole, and I started getting high again. I got pulled over and was sent back to prison for another two years for possession.

I did that, got out, did parole, got a good job, and bought a truck. But I started using again and lost everything. My wife of 13 years divorced me and that killed me inside. That's when I woke up. That's when I knew I was an addict.

I was sitting in jail waiting to get into this meth program when the chaplain came around, and I turned my life back over to God.

I look back on my life and figured I can't do this anymore without God. I knew I needed help. I got a copy of the Yard Out from the chapel here and so much of the stuff in it really hit home. I would really like other people to turn their lives over to Christ as well. Thank you so much and God bless.

by Jeffrey in Michigan

The realization that you should not be in charge of yourself is an excellent first step towards your freedom as a believer in Jesus. Many people fear being out of control. There is a security created, albeit a false one, by feeling in control of all circumstances and situations. This often comes from deeply rooted fears of harm that was caused to you by others in authority over you. It is easy to be deluded into thinking you can control everything and everyone, that no one is the boss of you! However, that attitude is a fool's journey. The first principle in the Celebrate Recovery 12-step recovery program is "Realize I'm not God; I admit that I am powerless to control my tendency to do the wrong thing and that my life is unmanageable." (Step 1)

"Blessed are the poor in spirit, for theirs is the kingdom of heaven." Matthew 5:3
Even if your earthly Dad cannot see your progress, your Heavenly Father is delighted in His children when they obey and honor Him. That's for eternity!

"Road To Salvation" by Carlos in Michigan (made with acrylic on *"Stonehenge"* paper)

Nothing Is Going To Go Right With You

DAY 25

"Yet as for me, I know that my Redeemer lives, And at the last, He will take His stand on the earth." Job 19:25 NASB

My mom often said, "Son, until you get right with God, nothing is going to go right with you." I was arrested in November 2001, and I knew she was right. I was going to do time. I was miserable, angry, and depressed. I was at the end of my road, facing the fact that I had accomplished nothing worthwhile in life, and I was at a dead end.

I didn't know which way to turn, and I'm not talking about trying to get out of prison time. That was far from my mind. In the county jail, I was placed in a three-man cell with two Christian men. I wondered what they were about. They never directly witnessed to me, but I watched them closely all the time, not knowing it was going to affect me so drastically. The Holy Spirit began working on me, and I was in a constant state of confusion.

It didn't help matters that I was angry with God and wanted nothing to do with Him. My first daughter, Brittany Nicole, had died ten years earlier when she was only eight days old. I was hurt and wanted answers to why she had to die. I couldn't get any answers from preachers, and this just angered me all the more.

I began to look at God as cruel — a manipulating creator who sat around with Satan playing a giant chess game, with humans as the chess pieces. I even used the book of Job to prove my point about His great game. Boy, was I messed up. I had all these feelings about God, on top of my messed-up life.

On December 12, 2001, I stood alone in my cell. The Holy Spirit gripped me and made me stop all thoughts and feelings. At that very moment, the full realization of my sins overflowed my heart. I broke down completely, and confessed my sins, begging Him to come into my heart and make me clean and whole. Let me tell you, He did just that.

I've never said, "If you get me out of this mess, I'll do this or I'll do that." I never tried to use Him as a crutch to get out. Guess what? The first thing He did was answer my question about my daughter Brittany. The very nano-second God stepped through the door of my heart, He said, "My son, she was mine before she was ever yours." A smile came upon my face, and I was comforted and at peace for the first time in ten years.

From that moment on I knew what it meant to be truly alive. I was so dead in my sins. I was living a life of self-pride and seeking the pleasures of this world. I drank and partied and did other things. I was so blind, like I was being led around like a bull with a ring in his nose. The point is, I was caught up so much in the world of sin that I couldn't see it.

The Holy Spirit opened my eyes and showed me my sins. Once I repented and let God in my life, He made me whole. A peace entered me, and I've been full of joy ever since.

Yes, I'm in prison doing time, but I'm free. Freer than any bird that flies in and out of this prison compound. The Spirit in me won't let me see those fences and razor wire. Walking with Christ is all that matters. It is the best feeling you can have. I wouldn't trade it for all the riches in the world. If you just open your heart, He can do the same for you.

By Michael in Florida

It can be difficult to grapple with losses and devastation in life. The book of Job is rich with philosophical discussions between Job and his well-meaning friends who try to comfort Job with their futile understanding of God. Job keeps his faith in the midst of devastating circumstances and unwise counsel (Job 19:25). Michael in Florida learned through his own journey what Job's friends found out in chapter 38, that God is in control. We cannot fathom His ways, but we can trust that He is good and we can rest in His promise that in all things, God works for our good (Rom 8:28).

"Grandma's Prayer" by Sally in Nevada

Becoming Useful

DAY 26

"I appeal to you for my son Onesimus, whom I have begotten while in my chains, who once was unprofitable to you, but now is profitable to you and to me." Philemon 10-11 NKJV

God has helped me all throughout my life. You couldn't have told me that 10 years ago. I felt that God was against me. How could He love me when my life felt like hell? April 23, 2008, I was sentenced to 60 months in the Florida DOC. I was numb and in denial thinking God had let me down again.

While I was in the holding cell, I asked why. It was then I realized that my life was surrounded by sin. How could Jehovah help me when the fruits I had were resentment, anger, and hate?

I started to cry as I was brought down to a low point in my life, not realizing that this point was all God wanted for me. He can't help us when we're in pride, when we have hate in our hearts. We must become as little children, humble, and (with) a desire to change.

Ever since I made a dedication to God to seek Him wholeheartedly, and learn His ways, I've experienced a change in what I used to believe. He has helped me seek advice before making any decisions.

What would Jesus do? I always ask myself this. His Word is so powerful and true that it can make the hardest heart turn into good. So that has helped me in more ways than one, to forgive, let go, and trust in Him.

I hope my words can bring encouragement and strength because just like God has helped me, He's always ready to help you too.

By Seville in Florida

The Apostle Paul wrote a heartfelt letter to a fellow believer named Philemon on behalf of a man who was in trouble and running from God. The man, Onesimus, had repented of his sin and was eager to make amends. The name "Onesimus" in Greek means "useful," and Paul had fun with the meaning; where Onesimus was once "useless," now, through Christ, he lives up to his name (Philemon 11). Indeed, Onesimus was very useful for the Kingdom, as he delivered the letters of Ephesians and Colossians from Paul. Brandon in Tennessee has caught the same vision as Onesimus—being useful for the Kingdom.

Have you run from God and His purpose for you?
In what ways can you now be "useful" for the Kingdom?

"Changing The Nature Of The Beast" by Paul in Kansas (made with acrylic on bristol board)

Take Me To The Hospital

DAY 27

"For 'whoever calls on the name of the Lord shall be saved.'"
Romans 10:13 NKJV

In late 2013 a friend shot me up with a needle full of crystal meth. My heart raced, ready to burst out of my chest. Boom-boom-boom was the sound of my near-death, beating heart. Immediately my body was frozen like a Popsicle.

All I kept saying was, "You put too much in. You shot me up with too much. Take me to the hospital!" My friend got me out of his house as far as my noodle legs could go. (Then) I heard my last heartbeat and—boom—I died.

My friend left me on the sidewalk some ways from his house. In my last moments, I was pleading, "Please, Jesus, please. God please, give me a second chance. My kids, my mom, my family. I'll tell everyone my story."

The only Scripture I could remember off the top of my head was, "For whosoever shall call upon the Lord shall be saved." I said a final, "Jesus, please."

Instantly, the breath of life kicked into me. Jesus—the same Jesus who raised Lazarus from the dead, raised me from the dead.

Since then, I have not used the needle again. But now, because I did continue my lifestyle of crime and gambling, I am happy to be incarcerated, because Jesus has His hand on me.

My life is not mine, but His and His alone. This is my story and God wants all of us in His story, for His glory.

By Marie in Hawaii

Marie all but died, abandoned for dead. God, in His great kindness, answered her pleading and revived her from physical death. Still, He wasn't through. In His mercy, God showed Marie a second great kindness that day. He opened her eyes to her own spiritual death.

Scripture paints us all as spiritually dead when we enter this world, separated from God here and forever because of our sin. "For whoever calls on the name of the Lord shall be saved.'" (Rom.10:13) Jesus offered His life on a cross to take God's wrath toward our sin. Through faith in Him, we all can be truly revived—to spiritual life.

Have you passed from spiritual death to eternal life?

Oh! How precious life is in God's eyes!
For He uses women as vessels to life.
How grateful we should all be...
For He provides so many
wonderful rewards.

LITTLE WONDERS

"LO, CHILDREN ARE AN HERITAGE OF
THE LORD; AND THE FRUIT OF THE WOMB
IS HIS REWARD. — PSALMS 127:3

"Little Wonders" by David in Georgia

Changed Way Of Thinking

DAY 28

"Do not conform to the pattern of this world, but be transformed by the renewing of your mind. Then you will be able to test and approve what God's will is—his good, pleasing and perfect will." Romans 12:2 NIV

I'm serving 16 to 40 years for driving under the influence and causing a death. I've been incarcerated since 2015 and have fought to have my sentence restructured. Along this journey have been some tough times. I was involved in a Las Vegas gang and all the things I did while incarcerated the first time are now catching up to me.

I was first incarcerated at the age of 14 and was certified as an adult. While doing that bid, I was involved in a lot of institutional violence due to my gang involvement. After 13 1/2 years, I was released and never thought about coming back. As you can see, I'm back and I'm now searching for God and the peace that comes with it. I'm in a lock down unit at the moment and have written a kite to receive a Bible. Along with it came a Yard Out newspaper. So, I'm reading the material and am thinking, "Why not reach out and speak my testimony?"

I just want to say to anyone who is going down the wrong path, please allow the help from God or anyone who is offering. I've spent over half my life fighting this fight and I'm now 39 years old. Please don't lose your life to the system the devil has infiltrated in our communities, our minds, or our hearts.

I have finally given myself the opportunity to change my way of thinking and allowing God to help me embrace the new me. I wasn't this comfortable until I was in this cell and reflected on doing the wrong things that got me nowhere but heartache and pain.

I allowed God to take me on HIS journey. So, please, to the adults and kids who get to read this, as long as you're breathing, it's never too late to change.

By Kenneth in Nevada

Once our way of thinking has been changed, everything we perceive changes. When we learn compassion, we perceive others struggles without judgment. When we learn grace, we are not as easily offended. When we learn patience, we navigate changes better. When we learn trust, we face disappointment better. These new attributes only come by the renewing power of the Holy Spirit. We who believe are continually being changed into the image of Jesus Christ. Our thoughts and ways are being changed to HIS thoughts and ways.

"Momma, Don't Stop Praying" by Helena in Texas

Learning To Love

DAY 29

"Each of you should use whatever gift you have received to serve others, as faithful stewards of God's grace in its various forms." I Peter 4:10 NIV

At nineteen years old, I was sentenced to ten years. I lost hope in everything. At a time when I should have been living it up, I was being locked down. I hated life and everything else too.

While I sat stewing in my misery, one female took the time to know me, to help me get out of my "hate-everything-and-everyone" attitude, and to slowly teach me how to love. Through her faith in God and constant invitation to go to church or do a one-on-one Bible study, I started to find my faith.

Leaning on God is the best decision I made. As my faith grew stronger and stronger, I recognized that this amazingly amazing woman had guided me back to God. If I did not learn to love and drop my walls, God and I wouldn't be in a close relationship today.

Finding the faith I have today helped me recognize the true power of God's love. My message to anyone who reads this is "Don't take advantage of those who are trying to lead you back to God. No matter how unfair life is, embrace all those (difficult) places in your path." God can truly heal you. He's the only one who can.

By Casey in Hawaii

Praise God that through His only son, God can truly heal. We all know those around us buried in their own quicksand of hopelessness, pain and anger. Every struggle against life just sucks them further and further into the pit. They need help out. Casey was blessed by a woman of faith who knew the power of Christ in her own life and wanted to share that healing power and love with a friend. That "amazingly, amazing" woman was used by God. She lived out her faith. She encouraged, challenged, forgave, and stayed faithful to Casey and to Christ. In the end, she helped heal a life.

Who in your life needs an "amazingly, amazing" person to guide him or her to the Savior? Could you be that person?

"Rescued, Not Arrested" by Richard in North Carolina

Prison Nights

DAY 30

"...Lord my God, I will give thanks to You forever."
Psalms 30:12 NASB

As I lay still in my prison bunk, am I the only one awake?
My heart is eager, oh, Dear Lord, until morning, I can't wait.
I really need to talk to you about something on my heart.
I have so much to say but Lord where do I start?
Let me first thank you, Lord, for this life you've given me,
And though I'm still in prison, my eyes are clear to see.
This isn't the plan you had for me. You had greater things in store.
But now I'm ready to follow you and choose to sin no more.
Sometimes you teach us lessons, Lord, though they may be hard,
In order to see your light, we must first flee from the dark.
You spared my life many times, you see the good in me.
And though I am a filthy rag, your blood has washed me clean.
Father, I come humbly before you, I'm down on hands and knees,
Praying that you touch a life just as you have touched me.
For those that may not know you, Lord, for those too blind to see.
May they see your power and glory through the change you made in me.

By Joy in Alabama

Awesome is the beauty of a redeemed life: eager, dependent, thankful, content. Eyes open wide to lost opportunities and shamelessly turn to follow Him. A redeemed life is clean and righteous in the blood of Christ, reflecting His humility and compassion.

*"You have turned my mourning into dancing for me;
You have untied my sackcloth and encircled me with joy,
That my [a] soul may sing praise to You and not be silent.
Lord my God, I will give thanks to You forever."*
Psalms 30:11,12 NASB

Have you ever met someone who radiates Jesus?

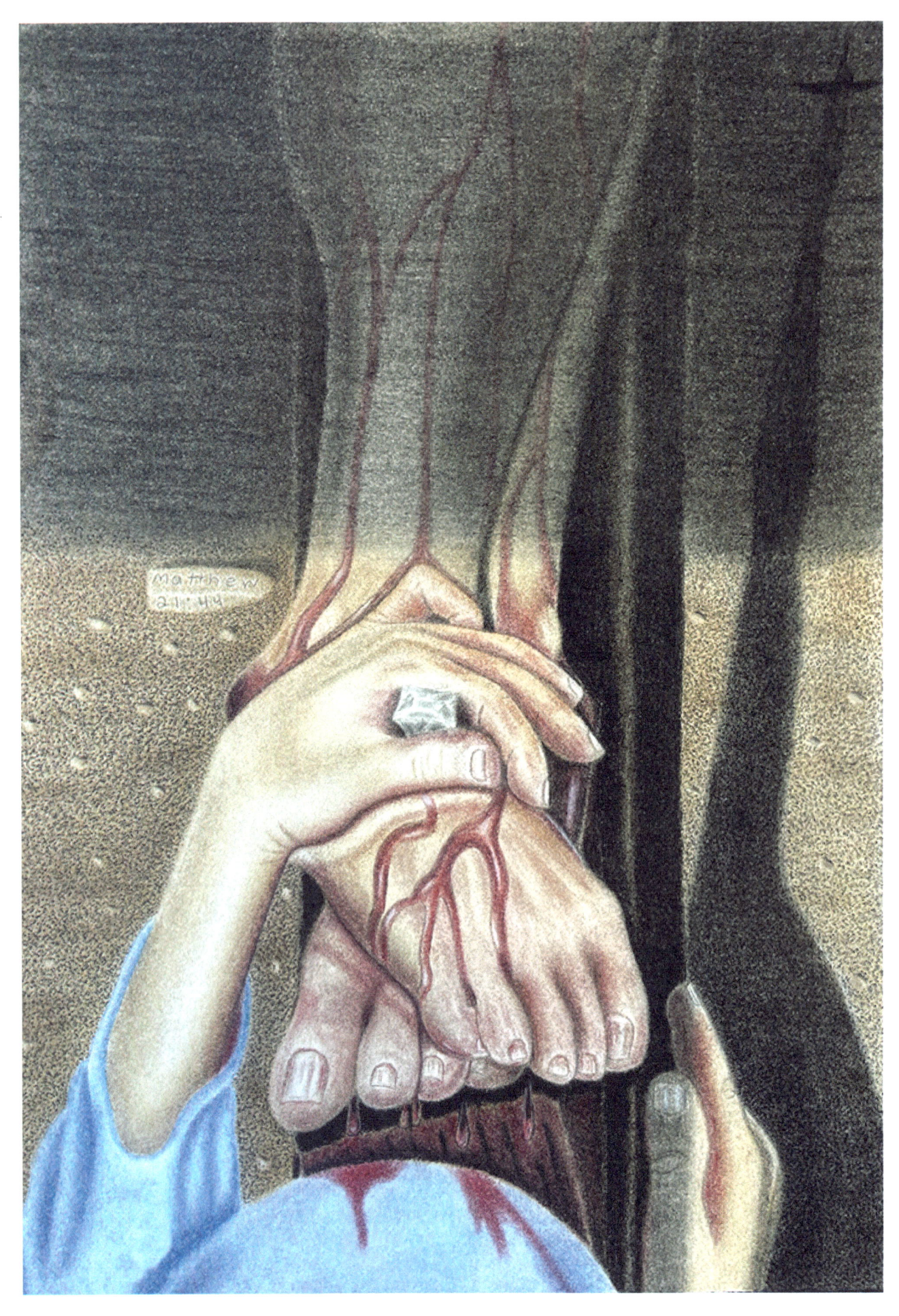

"At His Feet" by Charles in Michigan

Can I Get Through?

DAY 31

"Being confident of this, that He who began a good work in you will carry it on to completion until the day of Christ Jesus."
Philippians 1:6 NKJV

Guilty or not, the system has you. You're going down to face the hard reality of a world called, "Time." No person in their right mind could be happy about it. It means separation from the world as you know it, your loved ones, and your career.

The D.O.C.'s routine was set in motion long before you arrived and it will continue long after you leave. Like it or not, you will have to conform to it.

You're reminded of the consequences of your misdeeds every morning as you try to mentally escape the endless miles of cold steel bars and the unforgiving concrete. Frustration, anguish, and helplessness daily pushes a person to the limit of their endurance and tolerance.

Classification will hopefully assign you a meaningful job. There are education and rehabilitation concerns that should be addressed. You will eventually find supportive friends, yet even with these positive straws to grasp, there seems to be nothing surrounding you but fear and uncertainty.

There seems to be nobody who can totally help you. Fellow inmates offer solutions to all your problems, but even worse, their lives are in bigger shambles than yours! But you have not been stopped dead in your tracks for nothing. God has a reason for everything.

Don't be so set in your attitudes that you ignore the still small voice that continues every night as you try to sleep. There is no one to kid now. Some of your best scams and plans got you here. It's pretty obvious God had trouble getting your attention. Are you listening to Him yet?

You have a God who still listens if you take the time to ask. He's not there to just get you out of prison. He's the way to get you THROUGH prison.

Most important, seek God with everything within you. Your life and future depend on it. If you want something you've never had, so something you've never done before, **turn your life completely over to God.**

By Gene in Iowa

Gene in Iowa gives us a sobering reminder of how difficult, and sometimes hopeless, prison life can feel. Gene's letter was chosen to finish this devotional because of his heartfelt plea to all who read his letter, "...turn your life completely over to God." If you are reading this and have not yet made a commitment to follow Jesus, would you consider doing so? You don't have to do your time alone. Jesus will go with you, strengthen you, give you wisdom and forgiveness if you only believe. He promises that what He starts in you, He will be faithful to finish it (Philippians 1:6).

Prayer Journal

Use the following pages to write down your thoughts and prayers after each day's devotion.

"Pastor Prays" by Joseph in Massachusetts

"This is the confidence we have in approaching God: that if we ask anything according to his will, he hears us." 1 John 5:14 NIV

DAY 1

DAY 2

DAY 3

DAY 4

DAY 5

DAY 6

DAY 7

DAY 8

DAY 9

DAY 10

DAY 11

DAY 12

DAY 13

DAY 14

DAY 15

DAY 16

DAY 17

DAY 18

DAY 19

DAY 20

DAY 21

DAY 22

DAY 23

DAY 24

DAY 25

DAY 26

DAY 27

DAY 28

DAY 29

DAY 30

DAY 31

TRUE STORIES OF TRANSFORMATION

by: Peyton Burkhart, Yard Out Editor

Dear Reader,

Now that you've finished the Yard Out 31-Day Devotional, take a few minutes to think about the testimonials and inspirational art within the pages. Likely, you said "Amen" a few times while reading these miraculous accounts as God rescued and changed people in a positive way. Maybe you related to the circumstances of their lives.

All of the features in this devotional are true stories of transformation. They show drama, danger, damage, and deliverance. In turn, each article has an arch, a start and finish. They are journeys of healing and restoration. Violent images come to mind—a desperate act, a fractured life, a chance to elude justice and escape against the odds. It usually plays out with a guy ending up handcuffed in the back seat of a black and white cruiser.

These aren't one-dimensional stories. They are way bigger and more meaningful because they are personal. Each episode captures the eternal consequences of real people and choices they have made. The hurting and broken, desperate for an answer, crashed in their effort to find one. Such conflicts show that a battle for the soul of every subject was fought and won.

How many of the experiences do you share? Just some, or do you share more than a few? Hopefully, every Christian who read this devotional found added strength to build up their faith and enhance his or her communion with God. For any nonbeliever, perhaps your spiritual need for God actually became apparent. Should the inspiration impress upon you to make a similar commitment, a "Connect to Jesus" prayer is included here:

> "Lord God, I believe in you. Thank you for loving me and sending Jesus to rescue me by dying on the cross and raising alive from the grave. I'm sorry for all the dark and sinful things I've done. Please forgive me. Come into my heart, Jesus. I receive you as my Lord and Savior. Teach me your ways, fill me with the Holy Spirit, and help me stay true to you forever. Amen."

Yes, it is appropriate to say "Amen," but this isn't "the end." You are just getting started. Life with Jesus is a continuous journey—trusting, learning, serving, and following faithfully.

Ephesians 1:17-19, (I pray) "the God of our Lord Jesus Christ, the Father of glory, may give to you the spirit of wisdom and revelation in the knowledge of Him, the eyes of your understanding being enlightened; that you may know what is the hope of His calling, what are the riches of the glory of His inheritance in the saints, and what is the exceeding greatness of His power toward us who believe, according to the working of His mighty power."

Peyton Burkhart

"Perfected Praise" by Dreflian in Virginia

WRITE TO PFC TODAY!

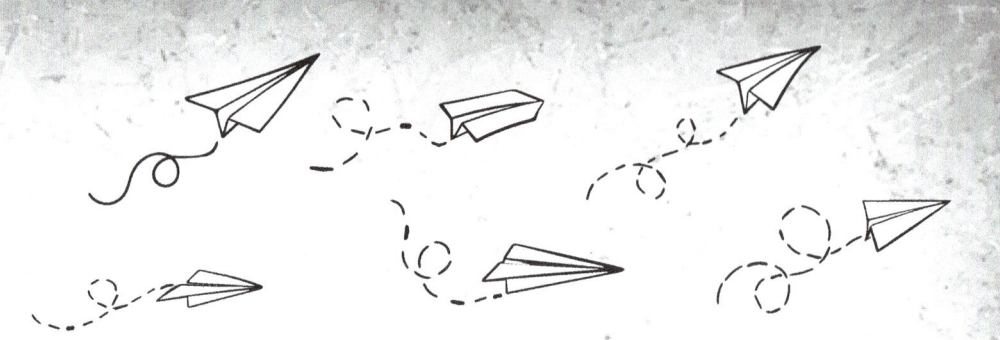

WE WANT TO HEAR FROM YOU! Let us know how you're doing; send us your prayer requests; ask us for free resources ; let us know your thoughts on this devotional and/or The PFC Study Bible; send your testimonies and artwork to "Attn: Yard Out" at PFC's address. WRITE US TODAY!

Yard Out Newspaper

Bible Study Correspondence School

Edifying Brochures

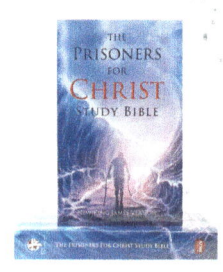

The Prisoners For Christ Study Bible

Books written by PFC's President & Founder, Pastor Greg Von Tobel:

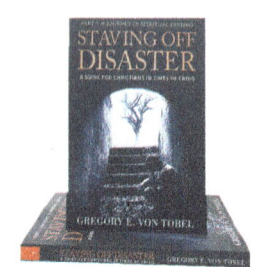

Staving Off Disaster: A Personal Journey Through Biblical Fasting

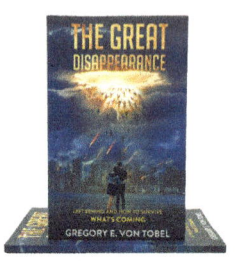

The Great Disappearance: Left Behind and How to Survive What's Coming

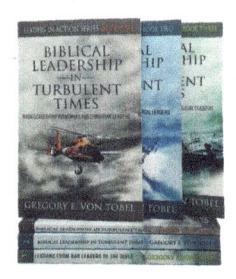

Biblical Leadership In Turbulent Times: Books 1-3

Prisoners For Christ
Outreach Ministries
P.O. Box 1530
Woodinville, WA 98072

Made in the USA
Monee, IL
01 July 2023